REED CONCISE GUIDE

WILDFLOWERS
of Australia

Ken Stepnell

NH

First published in 2015 by Reed New Holland Publishers

newhollandpublishers.com

A record of this book is held at the British Library and the National Library of Australia.

ISBN 978 1 92151 755 6

Managing Director: Fiona Schultz
Publisher and Project Editor: Simon Papps
Designer: Thomas Casey
Production Director: Olga Dementiev

Keep up with New Holland Publishers on Facebook
www.facebook.com/NewHollandPublishers

CONTENTS

Flower families

INTRODUCTION

Australian wild flowers

Australia's flora is very special. The famous botanist J.D. Hooker wrote that the country contains more unique plant species than any other place of a similar size. Upwards of about two-fifths of the genera and about seven-eights of the species in Australia are not found anywhere else around the world.

The flora in Australia is renowned for its richness and variety. The primitive appearance of many of the plants is strangely fascinating, as well as the areas in which they grow. Some favour small cracks in between rocks and live in complete solitude, while others make a carpet of colour in the vast inland region of Australia. Mountain areas can also become a blaze of colour when species such as Snow Daisy are in bloom.

Special adaptations

A great number of Australia's native flowers are xerophytes (drought-resistant) and these can be identified by their hardy leaves which are stiff, leathery and sharply pointed or divided. Many native flowers prevent water-loss through a covering of soft hairs, wax or cuticles, which protect them to some extent, without cutting off the air supply, hence the grey-green colour of much of our flora's foliage.

In areas where the soil is open, the water remains for only a short time around the roots. Many of the plants have thick fleshy leaves and the plant stores water in these for later use. Some plants, including native orchids, can live and thrive for over a year without water.

The seeds of many plants will stay dormant for years in the soil until conditions are suitable for regeneration, usually after fire. These plants flower profusely for some years, then disappear only to resurface later when the cycle is repeated. Many species of native orchids and flowers appear only after fire, then all traces of them are lost until the next fire. So in certain cases fire is not always a bad thing for our plants.

Threats

Unfortunately many of our plants have disappeared over the years, either nationally or locally, often due to land-clearance for development or too many bush fires. Experts believe that over 70 species of plants have been lost since Australia was settled and over 200 species of plants are on the endangered list.

No doubt each day the threat becomes worse. Settlement and progress cannot be blamed entirely for the loss of species. Alien species, introduced both by accident and on purpose, have become a threat to native flowers in many areas. Hopefully increasing public awareness and pride will help to control the spread of these plants that are now called weeds. The Field Naturalist Groups and the Society for Growing Native Plants are just two of the organisations that have encouraged home gardeners to plant their own native gardens.

To some travellers, just seeing a variety of native flowers on a roadside verge has been enough to convert them into being a flower lover. Unfortunately, in many areas these are now the only places where native flowers can be found in any great numbers; progress has overtaken species that were growing on farms or in bush land. Crown lands or national parks will contain many species of native flowers, and perhaps these areas may be the 'saviour' for some of our plants.

Wild flower highlights

In the eyes of many people Western Australia is the jewel in the crown in terms of native flora, and to botanists it is known as 'the wildflower state'. After some of the early explorers thought it was an uninspiring place, the likes of Von Muller and his botanists proved that it was unique in terms of the variety of plants that could be found. This is still the case today.

More and more people are becoming interested in plants, both for relaxation and enjoyment. It is hoped that this may slow the rate of destruction of many of the world's endangered plants and habitats. Tourism is also helping to make people from all walks of life aware of our native flowers, and this has helped with many varieties of native plants now being grown in nurseries around Australia.

I hope that this guide will help the dedicated nature enthusiast and the next generation of flower lovers to appreciate the enormous variety of special plants that are found in our country. The words and descriptions will hopefully be of use to everyone, including beginners. Hopefully it will contribute towards more people appreciating nature in all its glory.

The species in this book.

As much as possible this guide attempts to cover common and widespread species, and it also includes some of the specialities from particular regions, states, territories or habitats.

The flowers are listed in taxonomic order by family. The order broadly follows the APG (Angiosperm Phylogeny Group) III system of flowering plant classification, which is a modern, mostly molecular-based, system.

The Latin name is listed alongside the common name. It is a must for all people who are interested in flora to use these botanical names. Common names are not always universally applied and there are still some local and regional variations.

Each species account gives at least one photograph for identification and also a concise description of the plant's form, its leaves, flowers and other key identification features. The 'Habitat/Range' section is also of particular importance for ID, as a flower which is a speciality of one particular soil-type or region is unlikely to occur elsewhere.

THE FLOWERS

Christmas Bells *Blandfordia nobilis*

HEIGHT/ID: 80cm. An upright perennial plant, with a few leaves at the base of the stem – these are like grass and can be up to 80cm long.

FLOWERS: Red flowers are tipped with six yellow lobes. They are bell-shaped, up to 4cm long and 1cm wide. Usually arranged in sets of 3–10 flowers. Flowers from winter to spring.

HABITAT/RANGE: Prefers wet heathland and swampland of coastal New South Wales.

Purple Flags *Patersonia occidentalis*

HEIGHT/ID: 55cm. A small tufted perennial herb. Long, smooth and hairless leaves are shaped like a sword and grow to 55cm.

FLOWERS: Up to 7cm across. Blue or violet, they have three large and very conspicuous petals. Flowers in spring.

HABITAT/RANGE: Grows in most of the temperate areas of New South Wales, Victoria, Tasmania, South Australia and Western Australia.

Giant Boat-lip Orchid *Cymbidium madidum*

HEIGHT/ID: 40cm. Has long strap-like leaves and large seed-pods.

FLOWERS: The pendulous spray of these flowers, along with the fragrant perfume, are a characteristic part of the tropics. Flowers can be green to yellow, are about 3cm across and last about two weeks. Flowers from winter to spring.

HABITAT/RANGE: Grows on rotting logs and forks in trees in areas of tropical Queensland and New South Wales. Often found in rainforests.

Grassy Boat-lip Orchid *Cymbidium suave*

HEIGHT/ID: 70cm. One of the orchid species that grows into clumps. Stems are narrow, but are able to extend for some distance while growing.

FLOWERS: Colour varies from dark green to green or brownish, often they are blotched. Grow to 3cm across. The racemes are arched almost to the point of being pendulous. Flowers winter to spring.

HABITAT/RANGE: Hollow tree limbs, old tree stumps and rotting timber are favourite places for these orchids. Coastal areas of rainforest and tropical regions of Queensland and New South Wales.

Red Beaks Orchid *Pyrorchis nigricans*

HEIGHT/ID: 50cm. The fleshy leaf is rotund to ovate and is from 2–6cm wide.

FLOWERS: Each stout stem is usually from 2–6cm. Blooms are dark reddish in colour. The hood-like dorsal sepal is prominently striped with red or purple. Has spreading lateral sepals and the petals are linear. Flowers in spring.

HABITAT/RANGE: Grows in a variety of soils and conditions in Western Australia, South Australia, New South Wales, Victoria and Tasmania. Flowers well after fire.

Grampians Leafy Greenhood *Bunochilus macilentus*

HEIGHT/ID: 30cm. Stem is erect with sword-shaped leaves to 4cm long. The stem clasps the flowers and the leaves are arranged in a rosette.

FLOWERS: As many as 10 blooms can occur on the stem. Flowers are light green, the dorsal tips have pale orange markings, and they occur in loose racemes. Flowers in spring.

HABITAT/RANGE: Moist and well-drained areas suit this species, which is found over much of Victoria.

Blunt Greenhood *Pterostylis curta*

HEIGHT/ID: 30cm. Perennial and erect. Leaves are flat, oval and tapered at each end. One flower per stem, stems can be 25cm tall.

FLOWERS: White with green stripes and often soft green all over. The middle sepal forms the hood, the other two sepals are slightly curled with the tip pointed. The lateral sepal is slightly pointed upwards, rarely above the hood. Flowers in spring.

HABITAT/RANGE: Coasts and any moist areas of Victoria, New South Wales, Tasmania and South Australia.

Alpine Greenhood *Pterostylis alpina*

HEIGHT/ID: 40cm. Perennial and erect. Leaves are oval, flat and tapered at the end; they can be up to 4cm long.

FLOWERS: Pale green flowers, usually to 3cm long. The labellum tip protrudes a short distance through the flower. The dorsal sepal is blunt-tipped and the sepal points curve backwards. Flowers in spring.

HABITAT/RANGE: Not strictly alpine and occurs at different altitudes throughout the high country of New South Wales, Victoria and Tasmania.

Nodding Greenhood *Pterostylis nutans*

HEIGHT/ID: 30cm. Perennial and erect. Leaves are flat, oval and pointed at the end.

FLOWERS: White with some green stripes, can often be green with white on the bonnet. The hood on the bonnet is formed by the middle sepal, other sepals are bent towards the tip and sometimes curved. Flowers in spring.

HABITAT/RANGE: Found in heathland, open forest country, both wet and dry forests and coastal areas of Victoria, New South Wales, South Australia, Tasmania and Queensland.

Blotched Cane Orchid *Thelychiton gracilicaulis*

HEIGHT/ID: 10cm. Thin, notched leaves which are yellow to greenish.

FLOWERS: From 5–10 flowers about 1.3cm across. Flowers often droop. They are often yellow with large reddish or brown spots on the outside. Sepals and petals spread and slightly incurved, they are thick and partly fleshy. Flowers winter to spring.

HABITAT/RANGE: Rainforest, moist areas and humid areas of Queensland and New South Wales.

Scarlet Greenhood *Diplodium coccinum*

HEIGHT/ID: 30cm. Leaves are arranged in a rosette and are sword-shaped. They are large and often bluish-green. Labellum long and protruding.

FLOWERS: Deep maroon to reddish flower, but can also be green with a brown tip. Usually the flower leans forward, with only one flower per stem. Flowers in summer.

HABITAT/RANGE: Grasslands and open forest areas of New South Wales, Victoria, Queensland and Tasmania.

Swamp Greenhood *Diplodium tenuissimum*

HEIGHT/ID: 30cm. A slender stem and a few small, thin, dark green leaves. Labellum is lance-pointed and curved.

FLOWERS: Small and slender on the stem, not quite 1cm wide. Nearly white with green markings. They are slightly curved, the dorsal sepal has a long thread-like apex. Flowers spring to summer.

HABITAT/RANGE: Prefers swamp areas, in particular under Woolly Tea Tree, in areas of Victoria and South Australia.

Jug Orchid *Stamnorchis recurva*

HEIGHT/ID: 45cm. A leafy stemmed plant, unusual because it has the horned lateral sepals more prominent than the hood.

FLOWERS: Large and jug-shaped flowers, which can be several centimetres long. They are greenish with white stripes and red to brown points. The labellum is enclosed in the flower. Flowers in spring.

HABITAT/RANGE: Found from Geraldton to Israelite Bay in Western Australia.

Boorman's Rustyhood *Oligochaetochilus boormanii*

HEIGHT/ID: 20cm. Leaves set in a rosette.

FLOWERS: May have up to eight blooms – each 1.3cm in diameter – these hang forward as though they are nodding. The labellum is thick and broad, while the lateral sepals are turned down and flare from the base. Dorsal petal long and pointed with incurved edges. Flowers are reddish-brown on a green stem. Flowers in spring.

HABITAT/RANGE: Found in a variety of regions, especially favours rocky areas of Queensland, New South Wales, Victoria and South Australia.

Bearded Greenhood *Plumatichilos plumosum*

HEIGHT/ID: 25cm. From 5–20 ground-hugging, fleshy and lance-shaped leaves.

FLOWERS: Very translucent green with dark green net marking usually shiny. The dorsal sepal point can be to 1–2cm long and is nearly always curved. Pale yellow thread-like labellum hangs out about 2cm and is covered with tiny hairs. Flowers winter to spring.

HABITAT/RANGE: Grows in open forest areas and some grasslands in New South Wales, Victoria, Tasmania and South Australia.

Slender Sun Orchid *Thelymitra pauciflora*

HEIGHT/ID: 40cm. Perennial. Stem erect. Has solitary leaf which is narrow, linear and partially channelled.

FLOWERS: From 1–5 blue flowers on the stem. Each is 2cm across and they sheath at the base of the stem. Flowers in spring.

HABITAT/RANGE: Open heathland and forest regions of Queensland, New South Wales, Australian Capital Territory, Victoria, South Australia and Tasmania.

Spotted Sun Orchid *Thelymitra ixioides*

HEIGHT/ID: 60cm. Erect perennial. Leaves narrow and up to 20cm long.

FLOWERS: Usually blue, but occasionally pink or purple. Flowers are about 3cm across and often spotted black on upper petals. Several flowers per stalk. Flowers winter to spring.

HABITAT/RANGE: In forests, woodlands and coastal ranges of Western Australia, Queensland, New South Wales, Victoria and Tasmania.

Salmon Sun Orchid *Thelymitra rubra*

HEIGHT/ID: 42cm. Leaves are linear and about 11cm long. Bracts very narrow.

FLOWERS: About 2cm across, either one or two flowers per stem. Six petals, colour from salmon pink to pale pink. Petals and sepals egg-shaped. Flowers in spring.

HABITAT/RANGE: Coastal areas, heathlands and open forest areas of New South Wales, Victoria, Tasmania and South Australia.

Queen of Sheba *Thelymitra speciosa*

HEIGHT/ID: 30cm. Leaf can be twisted or spiral-shaped; base usually purple and can be blotched.

FLOWERS: From 1–5 flowers per stem. Colour is iridescent orange, purple, red or pink or variegated with a variety of shades, blotches or some streaks.

HABITAT/RANGE: Grows among low shrubs on heathlands of southern Western Australia. Widespread but rarely seen. Requires warm microclimate.

Great Sun Orchid *Thelymitra aristata*

HEIGHT/ID: 80cm. Has a single leaf, which is leathery, linear and pointed; it is often bluish-green and can be spotted. Terrestrial and only apparent above ground-level during the spring or summer growth period.

FLOWERS: Flowering stems can have up to 40 blooms. Flowers deep blue, sometimes lilac, each up to 6cm in diameter, sometimes many blooms are open at once. Flowers in spring.

HABITAT/RANGE: Open forest country, woodlands and swamp areas of New South Wales, Victoria and Tasmania, including both King and Flinders Islands.

Daddy Long-legs Orchid *Caladenia filamentosa*

HEIGHT/ID: 45cm. Leaf is narrow, but erect and spreading and the tips droop.

FLOWERS: Flower segments are long and thin, yellowish, white or reddish. Sepals and petals are covered with fine glands, but none at the base of the column. Flowers in spring.

HABITAT/RANGE: Grows in a variety of different soil types. Areas of Queensland, New South Wales, Australian Capital Territory, Victoria, Tasmania and South Australia.

Pink Fairy Orchid *Caladenia latifolia*

HEIGHT/ID: 50cm. Small perennial. Leaf is small, lancelote, usually prostrate and grows to 18cm long. Underside of leaf is soft reddish. Stem is very erect and grows to about 40cm.

FLOWERS: Dark pink flowers up to 3cm wide. Flowers winter to spring.

HABITAT/RANGE: In open forest country and heathland of New South Wales, Australian Capital Territory, Victoria, Tasmania and Flinders Island. Subspecies from Western Australia is illustrated.

Clubbed Spider Orchid *Caladenia clavigera*

HEIGHT/ID: 20cm. Perennial. Stem erect and slender, with a solitary leaf which can be up to 18cm long and sword-shaped; the under-surface is spotted.

FLOWERS: Red and green flower usually about 5cm across, sepals are reddish with black ends. Labellum heart-shaped, green to whitish, and tips usually rounded. Flowers in spring.

HABITAT/RANGE: Found in a variety of habitats, but especially favours open forest areas of New South Wales, Australian Capital Territory, South Australia, Victoria, Tasmania and Flinders Island.

Large Spider Orchid *Caladenia longicauda*

HEIGHT/ID: 60cm. Usually in clumps of a few plants, but can also be solitary. Leaf up to 20cm long and 2cm wide and slightly hairy on upper surface. Lateral sepals can be 12mm wide.

FLOWERS: Spectacular white flowers grow to several centimetres across, the petals have long thread-like pieces hanging down. Labellum heart-shaped. Flowers in spring.

HABITAT/RANGE: Widespread over much of Western Australia, from Geraldton to Esperance, in open forest, bushland and heathland areas.

Dwarf Jester Orchid
Caladenia bryceana ssp. *bryceana*

HEIGHT/ID: 3cm. Leaf grows to about 1.2cm and can have reddish colour. Sepals and petals are short as well.

FLOWERS: Grow to around 2cm and may also have reddish tinge on petals. Labellum has a downward curve, which is green with a red apex. Flowers in spring.

HABITAT/RANGE: Very restricted distribution in the Stirling Ranges of Western Australia.

Tongue Orchid *Cryptostylis subulata*

HEIGHT/ID: 80cm. Leaves lanceolate, dark green to yellow on both sides. Leaves absent at flowering time.

FLOWERS: Green to yellowish flowers 5cm across, they occur in erect terminal racemes with several blooms. Both sepals and petals are yellowish. Flowers winter to autumn.

HABITAT/RANGE: Often found among rushes in swamp areas and damp regions of Victoria, Queensland, New South Wales, Tasmania and South Australia.

Flying Duck Orchid *Caleana major*

HEIGHT/ID: 35cm. Small and erect. Leaves narrow, sword-like and grow to 10cm.

FLOWERS: Dark reddish to brown, some may have green sepals and petals. Resembles a duck in flight – labellum is attached by a small claw and forms duck's head. Flowers winter to spring.

HABITAT/RANGE: Open heathlands, open forests and woodlands of Victoria, New South Wales, Queensland, Tasmania and South Australia.

Hyacinth Orchid *Dipodium punctatum*

HEIGHT/ID: 1m. Leafless herb with a dark and robust stem.

FLOWERS: Pale pink to a deep pink, often with dark spots. Flower up to 2cm across, spoon-shaped lip can have a white beard. Up to 40 or 50 flower-heads on one stalk. Petals and sepals are all free and spreading. Flowers in spring.

HABITAT/RANGE: Widespread in forests, dry open woodlands and coastal ranges in Victoria, Queensland and New South Wales.

King Orchid *Dendrobium speciosum*

HEIGHT/ID: Grows on host tree. Leaves up to 30cm long.

FLOWERS: Perfumed creamy-white to yellow flowers can be 3cm across. Limbs up to 70cm long, each has many flowers – up to 100 is not uncommon. Petals oblong and pointed. One of the best-known tropical orchids. Flowers winter to spring.

HABITAT/RANGE: Widespread in coastal areas and rocky habitats in Queensland, New South Wales and parts of eastern Victoria.

Pink Fingers *Petalochilus carneus*

HEIGHT/ID: 25cm. Stem erect and slender with a single leaf, which is broad, hairy and about 20cm long, as well as having a musky odour.

FLOWERS: White or pink, some may have a dark band on lower petal. Up to four blooms on the one stem. Dorsal sepal erect and the red-barred lip on flower is conspicuous. Flowers in spring.

HABITAT/RANGE: Open forest areas and grasslands of Queensland, New South Wales, Australian Capital Territory, Victoria, Tasmania and South Australia.

Purple Enamel Orchid *Elythranthera brunonis*

HEIGHT/ID: 15cm. Perennial with erect stem and very hairy solitary leaf with a spread of about 10cm.

FLOWERS: Rich purple and glossy, these are very striking in a bush setting. Flowers up to 3cm across, petal almost 1cm and usually curved, 1–2 flowers per stem. Flowers winter to summer.

HABITAT/RANGE: Grows in a variety of soils in south-west Western Australia.

Pink Enamel Orchid *Elythranthera emarginata*

HEIGHT/ID: 30cm. Solitary, hairy, oval-shaped leaf with a dark reddish-green base. Stem erect.

FLOWERS: Brilliant pink and glossy, they occur in clusters of up to three blooms 5cm across. Flowers can be blotched with dark red or purple. Flowers winter to spring.

HABITAT/RANGE: Grows in a variety of soils and conditions in southern Western Australia.

Scented Leek Orchid *Prasophyllum odoratum*

HEIGHT/ID: 80cm. Perennial. Solitary cylindrical leaf is present when plant in flower.

FLOWERS: Flowers up to 1cm across and well spaced with up to 10 per stem. Flowers greenish-brown with white or pink petals, the prominent labellum is white or brown. Flowers in spring.

HABITAT/RANGE: Grows well in poor, well-drained soils of South Australia and Victoria.

Dainty Blue China Orchid *Cyanicula amplexans*

HEIGHT/ID: 25cm. Leaf often prostrate and in most cases broad.

FLOWERS: Pale blue labellum with a white or light cream calli. Flowers triple-lobed, the centre lobe incurved and slightly shorter than the others. Flowers winter to spring.

HABITAT/RANGE: Occurs in open areas of scrub and woodland in south-west Western Australia.

Common Golden Moths *Diuris chryseopsis*

HEIGHT/ID: 30cm. Leaves are straight, as is the flower stem.

FLOWERS: Flowers yellow and can have some dark internal streaks. Up to four flower-heads can be found on each stem. The petals are almost horizontal to partly drooping. Flowers in spring.

HABITAT/RANGE: Favours moist soils. Found in open grassland areas, forest regions and swamplands in New South Wales, Victoria, Tasmania and South Australia.

Western Purple Donkey Orchid *Diuris daltonii*

HEIGHT/ID: 40cm. Two leaves which are about 0.5cm wide and folded.

FLOWERS: Dark purple flower-heads are about 3cm in diameter. Petals usually erect.

HABITAT/RANGE: Open forest and red gum areas of Victoria and South Australia.

Green Bird Orchid *Simpliglottis cornuta*

HEIGHT/ID: 5cm. Leaves usually about 0.3cm wide.

FLOWERS: Colour of flowers varies from green to reddish-green and the petals are incurved slightly. The labellum is erect and heart-shaped, and the tip is often reddish to brown. Flowers spring to summer.

HABITAT/RANGE: Widespread and still common in moist open forest areas of New South Wales, Victoria and Tasmania.

Common Elbow Orchid *Thynninorchis huntianus*

HEIGHT/ID: 15cm. Stem is very wiry and thin, colour varies from green to red.

FLOWERS: The flower-heads look like tiny insects and are greenish to reddish in colour.

HABITAT/RANGE: Grows in most types of soil in areas of New South Wales, Australian Capital Territory, Victoria, Tasmania and Flinders Island.

Small Helmet Orchid *Anzybas unguiculatus*

HEIGHT/ID: 3cm. Perennial. Stem short and erect. Flat and oval solitary leaf is green with a red-grey under-surface.

FLOWERS: Maroon flower about 1cm in diameter and hooded. One flower per stalk. Flowers autumn to spring.

HABITAT/RANGE: In a variety of areas of New South Wales, Victoria, Tasmania and South Australia.

Stately Helmet Orchid *Corysanthes diemenica*

HEIGHT/ID: 4cm. In some cases the leaf is almost as large as the flower, barely 2cm. The leaf is bright green on the top and underneath a silvery green.

FLOWERS: Flower has an almost bird-like profile, it is about 1.5cm in diameter. Petals can be erect or recurved – they are dark red with transparent mottles. Flowers winter to summer.

HABITAT/RANGE: Grows in a variety of soils, but often found in rotted leaf-mould areas of the bushland in Queensland, New South Wales, Victoria and Tasmania.

Purple Beard Orchid *Calochilus robertsonii*

HEIGHT/ID: 40cm. Leaves fully developed when the plant flowers – they are about 1.2cm, and not much larger than the flower.

FLOWERS: Petals brown to greenish in colour with fine purple stripes. Mauve or white labellum has hair-like structures that resemble a beard. Flower usually only lasts a few days. Flowers winter to spring.

HABITAT/RANGE: Found in parts of Victoria, Queensland, South Australia, Tasmania and Australian Capital Territory.

Rattle Beaks *Lyperanthus serratus*

HEIGHT/ID: 40cm. Erect stem appears a little stout. Solitary leaf is sword-shaped, pointed and grows to around 30cm.

FLOWERS: Green flowers tinged with yellow, brown or reddish. Can be 2cm in diameter with long narrow petals and a curved dorsal sepal. Up to eight blooms per stem. Flowers in spring.

HABITAT/RANGE: Grows in a variety of conditions in southern Western Australia and occurs mainly in the Gin Gin district.

Banded Bee Orchid *Diuris laxiflora*

HEIGHT/ID: 8cm. A slender member of its genus with narrow and straight leaves.

FLOWERS: Yellow with dark blotches scattered over the flowers. Petals are erect and can be recurved. Flowers can be 2cm across. Flowers winter to spring.

HABITAT/RANGE: Found in grassland areas and some open forest country of Western Australia.

Common Potato Orchid *Gastrodia sesamoides*

HEIGHT/ID: 20cm. Flower stem is tall, slender, brown, fleshy and smooth.

FLOWERS: Tubular in appearance, usually light brown to whitish and with a slight fragrance. The flowers are bell-shaped and hang in loose racemes, which are usually 2cm long. Stem can have upwards of 25 flowers. Flowers in summer.

HABITAT/RANGE: Prefers damper areas of wet forests and mountain ranges of New South Wales, Victoria, Australian Capital Territory and Tasmania.

Erect Pencil Orchid *Dockrillia racemosa*

HEIGHT/ID: 120cm. Named because of its long cylindrical leaves. The long branched stems are initially erect and become pendulous as they grow.

FLOWERS: The slender white or yellowish-white flowers are about 2.5cm across. The flowers are not crowded on the stem like many other native orchids. Flowers in spring.

HABITAT/RANGE: Always associated with mountain or rainforest areas where conditions are cool and moist.

Streaked Rock Orchid *Dockrillia striolata*

HEIGHT/ID: 20cm. Leaves erect and pendulous and can be curved and often slender in appearance. The plant has a few small branches and the roots are open.

FLOWERS: Colour varies from creamy-yellow to greenish-brown. Up to 12 flowers per stalk. Flowers in spring.

HABITAT/RANGE: Occurs on rocks and sandstone cliffs in parts of New South Wales, Victoria and Tasmania, as well as on both Flinders and Cape Barren Islands.

Fragrant Tea-tree Orchid *Cepobaculum semifuscum*

HEIGHT/ID: 40cm. Leaves on the upper node are usually dark green. Racemes are up to 40cm long.

FLOWERS: Up to 20 yellow to brownish flower-heads with twisted shiny dorsal petals. Labellum narrow and slightly scented. Flowers about 3cm in diameter. Flowers winter to spring.

HABITAT/RANGE: Grows in forest and woodland on the trunks of melaleuca trees. Occurs in humid areas of north Queensland.

Banded Tree Spider Orchid

Tetrabaculum tetragonum

HEIGHT/ID: Grows on host tree and usually hangs downwards. Has a number of leaves, which typically are dark green.

FLOWERS: Greenish to yellow with narrow dark brown bands. Dorsal sepal very erect and can be 10cm long. Flowers winter to spring.

HABITAT/RANGE: Most commonly found growing on trees or rocks, and often near water. Occurs in coastal and mountain areas of New South Wales and Queensland.

Bonnet Orchid *Cryptostylis erecta*

HEIGHT/ID: 12cm. Leaves sword-shaped can be up to 3cm across.

FLOWERS: Flower stems can be 10cm and have up to 12 flowers per stem. Greenish to lilac flower about 1.5cm in diameter. Labellum egg-shaped with pointed tip and dark red markings and forms part of bonnet or hood on flower. Flowers winter to autumn.

HABITAT/RANGE: Found in a variety of soil-types in Queensland, New South Wales and Victoria.

Pink Spiral Orchid *Spiranthes australis*

HEIGHT/ID: 45cm. Dark green shiny leaves about 1cm across – they are erect, partly sword-shaped, and form a rosette.

FLOWERS: Stem can be 45cm high and have more than 50 flower-heads arranged in a spiral. Flower usually bright pink with a white labellum. Dorsal sepal and petals overlap to form a tube. Flowers in summer.

HABITAT/RANGE: Most types of soils in open country, marsh, swamps and high rainfall areas of Queensland, Australian Capital Territory, New South Wales, Victoria, South Australia and Tasmania.

Fairy Bells *Sarcochilus ceciliae*

HEIGHT/ID: Lives on host tree. Leaves heavily pigmented and very fleshy. Thick root seeks out any crevices for moisture.

FLOWERS: Light pink or magenta flowers usually 1cm in diameter. Up to 30 flowers can be in bloom at once. Flowers in spring.

HABITAT/RANGE: Rocky areas and mountain ranges of Queensland and New South Wales. This is one of 14 *Sarcochilus* species in Australia and they only bloom in high rainfall areas on the east coast.

Large Boulder Orchid *Sarcochilus hartmannii*

HEIGHT/ID: 20cm. Grows in clumps. Plant is branched and has numerous thickly textured leaves on each stem.

FLOWERS: Numerous flowers crowd each stem. They are usually white with crimson and yellow centres, but can occasionally be all white. Flowers in spring.

HABITAT/RANGE: Grows on rocks and cliff faces in areas of Queensland, and New South Wales. Favours cool areas but needs some sun.

Green Antelope Orchid *Ceratobium dalbertisii*

HEIGHT/ID: Lives on host plant. Usually has green to yellow leaf. Stem is erect, can be dark green and is partly notched.

FLOWERS: A white flower with green petals, often curved to one side. Labellum mainly white with pale purple stripes. Flowers are long lasting. In flower from March until December.

HABITAT/RANGE: Very local in occurrence and found on high branches of rainforest trees in Queensland.

Wax-lip Orchid *Glossodia major*

HEIGHT/ID: 15cm. Deciduous. Has a very slender erect stem with a single dark green leaf at ground-level.

FLOWERS: Five-petalled flower usually purple, but also occasionally mauve and rarely white. Labellum white and mauve. Dorsal sepal mostly erect, but can sometimes be curved. Flowers late winter to spring.

HABITAT/RANGE: Grows in a variety of soils and conditions in Queensland, New South Wales, Australian Capital Territory, Victoria, South Australia and Tasmania.

Cooktown Orchid *Vappodes phalaenopsis*

HEIGHT/ID: 45cm. This epiphytic plant is native to north Queensland. The leaves are mainly ovate, ribbed and green.

FLOWERS: A very distinctive orchid. Flower colour is most frequently pink, but can sometimes be lilac or white. Some flowers have a white spot on the lip. Long branches contain many flowers, each about 4cm in diameter. Flowers from summer to autumn. The floral emblem of Queensland.

HABITAT/RANGE: From coastal areas to mountain ranges in Queensland.

Blotched Sun Orchid *Thelymitra benthamiana*

HEIGHT/ID: 40cm. Broad leaf is light green to yellow.

FLOWERS: Several yellow to greenish-yellow flowers with many dark or reddish spots on the petals. Flower up to 4cm in diameter. Flowers in spring.

HABITAT/RANGE: Grows in a variety of soils from open forest areas to heathlands of Western Australia, South Australia, Victoria, Tasmania and Flinders Island.

Leafless Parson's Bands *Eriochilus cucullatus*

HEIGHT/ID: 15cm. A ground-hugging plant. Grows from a single grey-green leaf which is usually ovate and can be up to 2cm long.

FLOWERS: From 1–3 delicately perfumed flowers on the same stem. The species is distinguishable by the two deflexed lateral sepals, which are usually longer and can be white or pale yellow. Flowers from summer to autumn.

HABITAT/RANGE: Occurs in open forest and grasslands of Queensland, New South Wales, Australian Capital Territory, Victoria, Tasmania and South Australia.

Nodding Blue Lily *Stypandra glauca*

HEIGHT/ID: 1m. Erect perennial herb. Stem-clasping leaves up to 15cm long and 1cm wide and arranged in opposite rows along the stem.

FLOWERS: Blue with six nodding stamens, yellow filaments hang loosely in branching clumps at the ends. Flower diameter 2cm. Flowers from spring to summer.

HABITAT/RANGE: Widespread in a variety of soils and conditions in Queensland, New South Wales, Victoria, South Australia and Western Australia.

Blue Tinsel-lily *Calectasia cyanea*

HEIGHT/ID: 1.5m. Very upright perennial with wiry stem. Leaves narrow and pointed, 3–5mm long and 1mm wide.

FLOWERS: Blue or deep purple flower is a five-pointed star, 10cm in diameter, with six protruding yellow stamens. Flowers from winter to spring.

HABITAT/RANGE: Prefers the well-drained sandy and forest areas of Victoria, South Australia and Western Australia.

Black Gin *Kingia australis*

HEIGHT/ID: 2m. Erect perennial with broad solitary trunk. Grey-green grass-like leaves to 60cm long; very hairy when plant young.

FLOWERS: Globular flower-heads cream to grey and grow from a stout stalk up to 50cm long. Flowers from winter to spring.

HABITAT/RANGE: Favours open heathlands in Western Australia.

Red-and-green Kangaroo Paw
Anigozanthos manglesii

HEIGHT/ID: 1m. Leaves rise from sheath at base of the plant. Each is about 50cm long and 1cm wide.

FLOWERS: Green and red tubular flowers up to 10cm long. Usually has six curled black lobes on one side of the flower, the other side is covered with thick green hairs. Flowers from winter to spring. The floral emblem of Western Australia.

HABITAT/RANGE: Found in sandy bush and forest areas of Western Australia, and also in a small area of south-eastern Queensland.

Green Kangaroo Paw *Anigozanthos viridis*

HEIGHT/ID: 50cm. A perennial herb. Plant dies down in summer. Slender leaves can grow to 50cm long.

FLOWERS: Tubular flowers green or yellow-green, slightly split on lower side with reflexed lobes to 7cm long. Blooms from winter to spring.

HABITAT/RANGE: Open heathlands and forest regions of Western Australia.

Common Cat's Paw *Anigozanthos humilis*

HEIGHT/ID: 20cm. Small perennial herb. Leaves up to 20cm long; flat and sickle-shaped, usually die down when finished flowering.

FLOWERS: Tubular flowers up to 5cm long. Mainly yellow, suffused with red or pink. Single flowering stem is hairy. Flowers from spring to summer.

HABITAT/RANGE: Prefers sandy soils and open woodlands in south-west Western Australia.

Red Kangaroo Paw *Anigozanthos rufus*

HEIGHT/ID: 40cm. Perennial. Grows in a clump. Strap-like leaves grow to 40cm and often rather dull grey-green.

FLOWERS: Tubular flowers up to 4cm long. Usually brilliant red, sometimes purple. Flowering stems woolly and can be several centimetres high. Flowers from spring to summer.

HABITAT/RANGE: Occurs in low heath areas and open country in south-west Western Australia.

Black Kangaroo Paw *Macropidia fuliginosa*

HEIGHT/ID: 1.5m. Strap-like leaves rise from base of plant in sheath-like manner, they grow to 30cm long and 10cm wide.

FLOWERS: Striking in appearance – mainly black with a green tubular stem and up to 6cm long. They have six curled lobes on one side of the flower and are covered with tiny black hairs. Flowers from late winter to spring.

HABITAT/RANGE: Prefers the stony, gravelly, heath and mallee areas of south-west Western Australia.

Albany Synaphea *Synaphea polymorpha*

HEIGHT/ID: 50cm. A small shrub with a reddish stem, oblong in appearance and with undivided basal leaves to 20cm long. Upper leaves are much shorter with stiff points.

FLOWERS: Yellow flowers and have lobed petals. Individual flowers are about 1cm long. Flowers from spring to summer.

HABITAT/RANGE: Open woodland and bushland regions of eastern Western Australia.

Mountain Devil *Lambertia formosa*

HEIGHT/ID: 2m. A tall bush-like shrub. Leaves wedge-shaped and pointed, up to 2cm long, shiny green on upperside and off-white underneath.

FLOWERS: Red and tubular, 4cm long with a bearded interior. These are arranged in a small terminal cluster of seven flowers which is enclosed in a red bract. Flowers at almost any time of year.

HABITAT/RANGE: Prefers sandy dry soil of the forest and heathland of New South Wales.

Narrow-leaved Drumsticks *Isopogon anethifolius*

HEIGHT/ID: 2m. Usually an erect shrub, but in some areas can be almost prostrate. Leaves up to 10cm long, flat, stiff and divided into at least three linear-pointed or spear-pointed shapes.

FLOWERS: Stalkless yellow flowers occur in dense terminal globules. The rounded flower-heads are about 4cm across. Flowers from early spring to summer.

HABITAT/RANGE: Occurs in areas of New South Wales and Queensland.

Isopogon sp. *Isopogon latifolius*

HEIGHT/ID: 2m. Evergreen shrub, erect and usually stout in appearance. Leaves grow to 10cm long by 4cm wide; they are thick, broad, flat and slightly pointed.

FLOWERS: Purple or magenta flowers appear in terminal heads in a mass of tubular flower-heads. They are curved upwards to about 4cm and have small tufts of hair at the ends of the apex.

HABITAT/RANGE: Well-drained soils in south-west Western Australia.

Monga Waratah *Telopea mongaensis*

HEIGHT/ID: 2m. Open and upright shrub. Leathery leaves are linear, slightly curved and can be up to 15cm long.

FLOWERS: Red flowers about 10cm across in a terminal cluster – when in full bloom flowers appear to be flattened. Flowers in spring.

HABITAT/RANGE: In bushland and sheltered forest in New South Wales and Victoria.

Waratah *Telopea speciosissima*

HEIGHT/ID: 4m. Tall erect shrub. Leaves feel leathery and are narrow and oblong with serrated margins; they grow up to 25cm long and 4cm wide.

FLOWERS: Brilliant crimson-red tubular flowers with four curled lobes at the back and a white-tipped style at the terminal head. Flower-heads up to 15cm across. Flowers in spring.

HABITAT/RANGE: Coastal regions, mainly in the sandy soils of New South Wales and isolated areas of Victoria.

Prostrate Banksia *Banksia gardneri*

HEIGHT/ID: Prostrate shrub with strong, spreading, hairy branches. Linear leaves tend to be erect and stiff and appear from the base of the cone. Fully-grown sword-shaped leaves can be 40cm long and 8cm wide.

FLOWERS: Tubular flowers vary in colour from brown to soft yellow. Erect flower cone can be 10cm long and grows almost from ground-level. Flowers from spring into summer.

HABITAT/RANGE: Sandy heathlands of south-west Western Australia.

Silver Banksia *Banksia marginata*

HEIGHT/ID: Up to 10m; size depends on location. Can be a tall shrub, but often is only a small bush. Rough pale grey bark. Leaves narrow and obovate, dark green on top and off-white underneath, up to 5cm long and evenly spiked.

FLOWERS: Spikes can be 10cm long and 6cm across, usually pale yellow, styles also yellow. Flowers mainly in winter.

HABITAT/RANGE: Coastal heathland and open forest areas of Queensland, New South Wales, Victoria and Tasmania.

Scarlet Banksia *Banksia coccinea*

HEIGHT/ID: 5m. Multi-stemmed shrub with furry branches. Leaves are leathery to touch and oblong, can be 10cm long and 7cm wide, with some spikes on ends of leaves.

FLOWERS: Bright scarlet cylindrical spike up to 12cm long. Red styles tipped with a soft gold colour. Flowers from winter to summer.

HABITAT/RANGE: Light sandy soils and some gravel areas of south-west Western Australia.

Tennis Ball Banksia *Banksia laevigata*

HEIGHT/ID: 2m. A rather straggling shrub. Leaves are broad and linear, up to 10cm long with spikes on ends of leaves.

FLOWERS: Aptly named, the round flowers are the size of tennis balls and cream in colour. Flowers late spring to early summer.

HABITAT/RANGE: Restricted to a small area of southern Western Australia.

Woolly Banksia *Banksia baueri*

HEIGHT/ID: 4m. A thick and dense shrub. Leaves rigid and oblong, up to 15cm long and 2cm wide. They are evenly serrated with prickly margins and also veined. Also called Possum Banksia.

FLOWERS: When fully in flower the cones can be 24cm across and 20cm high. Colour resembles that of a teddy bear or possum. Flowers from winter into spring.

HABITAT/RANGE: Damp forest or woodland areas of Western Australia.

Hairpin Banksia *Banksia spinulosa*

HEIGHT/ID: 3m. Straggling but erect multi-stemmed shrub. Leaves 15cm long, narrow and linear with a prominent point and usually serrated edges.

FLOWERS: Small, tubular, cone-shaped flowers are bronze or honey coloured with black protruding styles on the cylindrical cone. Cones grow to 20cm long and about 6cm wide. Flowers from summer through to winter.

HABITAT/RANGE: Open forest country and most tableland areas of Queensland, New South Wales and Victoria.

Desert Banksia *Banksia ornata*

HEIGHT/ID: 2m. Well-rounded erect shrub, densely covered with limbs and leaves. Leaves tough in texture, up to 10cm long and 2.5cm wide, with serrated edges and a sharp point at tip.

FLOWERS: Plentiful yellow to bronze cylindrical flowers, up to 15cm long.

HABITAT/RANGE: Prefers desert, sandy soils and open forest, mainly in south-east South Australia and the south-west of Victoria.

Red Lantern Banksia *Banksia caleyi*

HEIGHT/ID: 2m. Erect shrub with fine bark on trunk and leaves scattered on the limbs. Leaves grow to 14cm long and have serrated edges.

FLOWERS: Flowers start off cream at the base then turn rich red; they hang down from the stem. Flowers from late spring to summer.

HABITAT/RANGE: Sandy soils in open woodlands and heath country of Western Australia.

Creeping Banksia *Banksia repens*

HEIGHT/ID: Prostrate shrub with erect leaves and many hairy horizontal branches which grow to 50cm long and 15cm wide.

FLOWERS: Pink-brown tubular cone-shaped flowers usually grow from ground-level; up to 15cm long and 6–7cm wide. Flowers from spring to early summer.

HABITAT/RANGE: Favours open sandy soils and heathlands, mainly in the Stirling Ranges of Western Australia.

Parrot Bush *Banksia sessilis*

HEIGHT/ID: 4m. Erect shrub. Leaves wedge-shaped, up to 5cm long and 3cm wide, with sharp prickles on the points.

FLOWERS: Pale yellow flowers in small terminal head which grows to 3cm long. These are surrounded by floral leaves and the short bracts are pale brown flowers. Flowers in spring.

HABITAT/RANGE: Common in jarrah forest and some coastal regions of Western Australia.

Golden Dryandra *Banksia nobilis*

HEIGHT/ID: 5m. Multi-branched shrub. Leaves up to 30cm long and 1.5cm wide with many small triangular sections on either side, dark green above and nearly white underneath.

FLOWERS: Orange to yellow flower-heads up to 7cm across, surrounded by floral leaves on short stem. Flowers from late winter.

HABITAT/RANGE: Woodlands in southern Western Australia.

Showy Dryandra *Banksia formosa*

HEIGHT/ID: 4–8m. Erect shrub or small tree. Branches covered with small hairs. Leaves narrow and linear and divided into many triangular lobes, edges lined with sharp needle-like thorns.

FLOWERS: Shiny yellow or orange with long hairy lobes and protruding styles, arranged in dense terminal head. Flowers in spring.

HABITAT/RANGE: Widespread in sandy heathlands of Western Australia.

Many-headed Dryandra *Banksia polycephala*

HEIGHT/ID: 4m. Tall and erect shrub. Leaves linear, up to 20cm long, recurved and well spaced with prickly lobes.

FLOWERS: Bright yellow heads up to 4cm across. Often many blooms on one branch. Flowers from winter.

HABITAT/RANGE: Woodlands and gravelly areas of south-west Western Australia.

Urchin Dryandra *Banksia undata*

HEIGHT/ID: 3m. Large and bushy shrub with hairy branches. Leaves egg-shaped and can be 10cm long and 6cm wide.

FLOWERS: Large golden flower-head has terminal heads, surrounded by clumps of floral leaves. Flowers winter to spring.

HABITAT/RANGE: Forest areas of south-west Western Australia.

Prickly Dryandra *Banksia falcata*

HEIGHT/ID: 4m. Erect loose shrub. Leaves up to 14cm long, alternated on stem, curled with long spines on edges. Branches have long brown hairs.

FLOWERS: From yellow to cream and faintly scented. Up to 40 flowers per stem. Flowers from winter to spring.

HABITAT/RANGE: A variety of habitats in south-west Western Australia.

Fuchsia Grevillea *Grevillea bipinnatifida*

HEIGHT/ID: 1.5m. Mainly a low and sprawling shrub, often prostrate. Limbs very hairy. Leaves rigid and prickly, growing to 20cm long and are divided into wedge shapes.

FLOWERS: Red flowers up to 15cm long with silky hair on outside. Flowers arranged in pendulous style, one side is spiky and resembles a spider.

HABITAT/RANGE: Harsh gravel and granite country in Western Australia.

Pink Pokers *Grevillea petrophiloides*

HEIGHT/ID: 2.4m. Tall and erect but spreading shrub. Leaves divided like 30cm-long needles.

FLOWERS: Pink to red cylindrical spike about 10cm long, sticky and with four curled back lobes.

HABITAT/RANGE: Prefers gravel or sandy soils in Queensland, Western Australia and Northern Territory.

Silky Oak Grevillea *Grevillea banksii*

HEIGHT/ID: 8m. Tall and spreading tree. Leaves divided, partly rounded and pointed. They can be 30cm long and are usually dark green.

FLOWERS: Usually cream-white, but can also be red or pink, they have a cylindrical spiked petal. Flowers from spring to summer.

HABITAT/RANGE: Widely distributed in coastal areas and open forests of Queensland.

Woolly Grevillea *Grevillea lanigera*

HEIGHT/ID: 2m. Mostly a rounded and hairy shrub. Leaves appear to be crowded on stem; they are linear, covered with soft hairs and can be up to 25cm long.

FLOWERS: Red flowers 6cm across with protruding styles and arranged in small clusters. Flowers can also be cream, green or pink. Flowers from spring to summer.

HABITAT/RANGE: Widespread in open woodland and gravelly or sandy areas of South Australia and Victoria.

Flame Grevillea *Grevillea eriostachya*

HEIGHT/ID: 2m. Very bushy shrub with stems that rise about 30cm above grey-green foliage. Leaf lobes very thin and up to 6cm long.

FLOWERS: Very colourful in flower. Greenish bud opens to a brilliant golden-yellow spike. A favourite with many nectar-loving birds. Flowers from spring to summer.

HABITAT/RANGE: Prefers dry sandy soils in Western Australia, Northern Territory and parts of South Australia.

Comb-leaf Grevillea *Grevillea pectinata*

HEIGHT/ID: 2m. Very erect shrub with divided pinnate leaves, which are loose, up to 3cm long and have a comb-like appearance.

FLOWERS: Usually deep red, but can be pink. They appear in clusters and follow no pattern on the shrub. Flowers in spring.

HABITAT/RANGE: Sandy loam or light gravel areas in southern Western Australia.

Mountain Grevillea *Grevillea alpina*

HEIGHT/ID: 1m. Sometimes this bush is prostrate, otherwise it is a low and spreading shrub and usually covered with hairy down. Leaves are soft, often crowded and dark green, up to 3cm long and 1cm wide.

FLOWERS: Usually red-orange, but can be green, yellow or pink, sometimes a combination of colours. Grampians form shown. Flowers from spring to summer.

HABITAT/RANGE: Favours sandy or open bush areas. Widespread in Victoria, occurs locally in New South Wales and South Australia.

Silver Grevillea *Grevillea parallela*

HEIGHT/ID: 10m. Tall shrub or tree with pendulous foliage. Leaves narrow and taper towards base, usually dull green above and covered with silky hair-veins on underside. Leaves may be divided into narrow lobes.

FLOWERS: Cream to white perfumed flowers are waxy, up to 10cm long, and crowded on cylindrical racemes. Flowers from mid-winter to summer.

HABITAT/RANGE: A variety of habitats in Northern Territory and Queensland.

Holly Grevillea *Grevillea aquifolium*

HEIGHT/ID: 4m. Can be prostrate, spreading or a tall shrub. Leaves up to 10cm long and to 4cm wide and can be oblong or ovate – they follow no pattern. They are often hairy, have some veins and can also be prickly.

FLOWERS: Colour varies – can be red, green or yellow. Racemes red, up to 5cm long and have no hairs. Flowers from spring to summer.

HABITAT/RANGE: Prefers light sandy open country in areas of Victoria and South Australia. One of eight species of grevillea in the Grampians.

Comb Grevillea *Grevillea huegelii*

HEIGHT/ID: 2.6m. A rigid, partly spreading and partly prostrate bush. Leaves stiff and divided into several pointed linear segments up to 2cm long and 2mm wide.

FLOWERS: Tubular and mainly red, sometimes pink and usually about 2.5cm long with four curled back petals. Flowers arranged in clusters. Flowers from spring to summer.

HABITAT/RANGE: Prefers light sandy soils and open bushland in areas of Western Australia, South Australia, Victoria and New South Wales.

White-plumed Grevillea *Grevillea leucopteris*

HEIGHT/ID: 3m. A very showy grevillea with many branches and pinnate leaves.

FLOWERS: White flowers hang on arched limbs and have a strong and unpleasant scent. Young buds covered with sticky pink bracts. Flowers from spring to summer.

HABITAT/RANGE: Sandy and heathland areas of Western Australia.

Grevillea sp. *Grevillea pinaster*

HEIGHT/ID: 4m. Trunk erect but looks straggling because of bushy branches which give woolly appearance. Leaves linear and silver-grey.

FLOWERS: Masses of deep pink or orange spider-like flowers appear in one-sided clusters which are up to 4cm long. Flowers winter to spring.

HABITAT/RANGE: Well-drained soil in open forest areas of south-west Western Australia.

Enfield Grevillea *Grevillea bedggoodiana*

HEIGHT/ID: 50cm. A spreading plant that is slightly prostrate. Leaves flat with sharp points along each edge, about 3cm across.

FLOWERS: Plum red or green flowers attached to the stem by short branches. Flowers can be single or in clusters. Flowers from spring to summer.

HABITAT/RANGE: Eucalypt forest in Enfield State Forest, Victoria.

Wickham's Grevillea *Grevillea wickhamii*

HEIGHT/ID: 4m. A very erect shrub. Leaves grey-green, flat, ovate, pointed and hairy, and up to 9cm long and 5cm wide.

FLOWERS: Red, orange or yellow flowers hang in clusters from main stalk. Flowers mainly in winter.

HABITAT/RANGE: Gravelly areas, limestone and spinifex country in Western Australia, Northern Territory and Queensland.

Long-style Grevillea *Grevillea longistyla*

HEIGHT/ID: 2.5m. Erect and open shrub. Branches silky, leaves linear and up to 25cm long.

FLOWERS: Red flowers in a loose cylindrical cluster. Racemes 10cm long, styles red and about 4cm long. Flowers from spring to summer.

HABITAT/RANGE: Sand plains, ridges and open forest areas of Queensland.

Coastal Hakea *Hakea clavata*

HEIGHT/ID: 2m. Spreading shrub with short brown branches. Leaves very succulent and slender.

FLOWERS: Rounded pale pink flowers in clusters about 3cm wide. Styles usually white and often smooth, can be 1cm or longer. Flowers mainly in winter.

HABITAT/RANGE: Coastal plains of south Western Australia.

Pincushion Hakea *Hakea laurina*

HEIGHT/ID: 3m. Spreading shrub with many branches, which at times are pendulous. Pointed leathery leaves are lance-shaped with prominent veins, up to 18cm long and 2.5cm wide.

FLOWERS: Light cream to begin, then turn crimson in a densely rounded ball of about 6cm. Cream to white styles protrude from centre of ball, these can be 2–3cm in length. Flowers in winter.

HABITAT/RANGE: Widespread on coastal plains of southern Western Australia.

Red Pokers Hakea *Hakea bucculenta*

HEIGHT/ID: 2m. An open and erect shrub. Leaves are linear and can be 20cm long and 2cm wide; they are flat and leathery to touch, with one central vein and a pointed tip.

FLOWERS: Red flowers in long spikes with racemes up to 18cm long. The style can be 2cm and slightly curved. Flowers from winter.

HABITAT/RANGE: Moist sandy soils and some areas of gravel surface in lower Western Australia.

Cauliflower Hakea *Hakea corymbosa*

HEIGHT/ID: 2m. A round-shaped shrub with short, hairy branches. Leaves are narrow and pointed, up to 8cm long and 8mm wide.

FLOWERS: Green to cream in colour, with dense clusters about 2.5cm across. They almost cover the shrub and the upper leaf axils are cream and smooth. Flowers in late winter to spring.

HABITAT/RANGE: Coastal areas, sand plains and mallee country in southern Western Australia.

Sea Urchin Hakea *Hakea petiolaris*

HEIGHT/ID: 2m. Erect shrub. Grey-green leaves are egg-shaped with pointed tip and prominent veins; up to 12cm long and 6cm wide.

FLOWERS: Cream at first then gradually turn pink to purple. The flowers grow to 5cm wide and are often found on the older wood or stalks. Flowers winter to autumn.

HABITAT/RANGE: Coastal areas and heathlands of Western Australia.

Snail Hakea *Hakea cristata*

HEIGHT/ID: 2m. A small, erect scrub. Leaves alternate along the trunk; they are up to 8cm long, egg-shaped, flat and have prickly edges.

FLOWERS: Slightly scented white flowers about 2cm across grow from the stem or trunk.

HABITAT/RANGE: Scrubland, sandy soils and granite outcrops in an area near Perth, Western Australia.

King Hakea *Hakea cucullata*

HEIGHT/ID: 4m. Open-branched shrub, with cupped, heart-shaped leaves up to 8cm across, which support the racemes of flowers.

FLOWERS: Buds enclosed by a broad silky bract. Flowers can be either red, pink or white. Flowers from late autumn to spring.

HABITAT/RANGE: Prefers the open heathlands of southern Western Australia.

Grass-leaved Hakea *Hakea multilineata*

HEIGHT/ID: 4.5m. Tall and erect shrub or small tree. Light green leaves are broad and linear, up to 20cm long and 1.5cm wide.

FLOWERS: From deep pink to red, in spikes up to 4cm long. Flowers from winter to spring.

HABITAT/RANGE: Grows in any type of soil and mainly in the south-west of Western Australia.

Long-leaved Petrophile *Petrophile longifolia*

HEIGHT/ID: 40cm. A ground-hugging plant with slender leaves.

FLOWERS: Silky flower-heads up to 6cm across are surrounded by many small pointed bracts. Flowers can be orange or yellow. Flowers from late spring to early summer.

HABITAT/RANGE: Prefers gravelly to limestone country and heathlands of Western Australia.

Hairy Jugflower *Adenanthos barbiger*

HEIGHT/ID: 45cm. Small erect multi-stemmed shrub. Flat green leaves up to 5cm long.

FLOWERS: Bright red, up to 4cm in diameter, with curled stamen at tip of flower. Flowers in spring.

HABITAT/RANGE: Common in sandy soils of south-west Western Australia.

Chittick *Lambertia inermis*

HEIGHT/ID: 3m. Straggling plant. Leaves are egg-shaped and pointed at tip.

FLOWERS: Can be orange or yellow. Flower-heads usually in clumps of seven. Styles up to 4cm long. Will flower at any time of the year if conditions suit.

HABITAT/RANGE: Open heathlands and gravelly areas near the south coast of Western Australia.

Common Smokebush *Conospermum stoechadis*

HEIGHT/ID: 1.5m. Erect and dome-shaped shrub, with many branches giving the plant a dense appearance. Slender leaves grow to 10cm long and are pointed at tip.

FLOWERS: Whitish-grey, from a distance can appear to be a shade of blue. They are woolly and tubular, growing to 8mm long. Flowers from spring.

HABITAT/RANGE: Open woodland and gravelly heathlands of Western Australia.

Cut-leaf Guinea Flower *Hibbertia cuneiformis*

HEIGHT/ID: 3m. Erect and bushy shrub. Leaves oblong and up to 4cm long, with some small prickles near the tip.

FLOWERS: The bright yellow flowers are prominent, 3–4cm across. Stamens are clustered into five bundles. Flowers from spring.

HABITAT/RANGE: Coastal districts of south-west Western Australia.

Spreading Guinea Flower *Hibbertia procumbens*

HEIGHT/ID: Prostrate to 40cm. A twiggy shrub with narrow stalks. Mainly prostrate and can spread to over 1m in diameter. Leaves small and dark with pointed tips and can be up to 2cm long.

FLOWERS: Bright yellow flowers bloom in great numbers at the ends of branches. Each flower has five petals and can be up to 10cm in diameter. Flowers from spring to summer.

HABITAT/RANGE: Prefers the open bushland areas and heathlands of Victoria, New South Wales and south-east Queensland.

Common Popflower *Glischrocaryon aureum*

HEIGHT/ID: 70cm. A tufted herb perennial with a very tough root system but no leaf system.

FLOWERS: A mass of yellow flowers hanging down in loose clusters from the numerous slender stems. Flowers in spring.

HABITAT/RANGE: Grows in a variety of soils and conditions. Most often found in the drier areas of Victoria, South Australia and Western Australia.

Pink Mulla Mulla *Ptilotus exaltatus*

HEIGHT/ID: 1m. Upright perennial herb. Leaves oblong and lanceolate; they can grow to 20cm long and 7cm wide with a thick tip at the end.

FLOWERS: Cone-shaped and lengthening to a cylindrical point; up to 25cm long and 5cm wide. Flowers deep pink and covered in a mass of silky hairs, but not on the tip of the flower. Flowers from winter to spring.

HABITAT/RANGE: Widespread across the arid inland of all mainland states. Flowers well after rain and appears to have no soil preference.

Black Bluebush *Maireana pyramidata*

HEIGHT/ID: 1m. Mostly a dome-shaped shrub. Stem can be hairy or smooth. Leaves very succulent and slender.

FLOWERS: Small and solitary greenish-yellow flowers with a shiny appearance. Flowers in spring.

HABITAT/RANGE: Widespread in the dry inland areas of all states of mainland Australia.

Batchelor's Buttons *Gomphrena canescens*

HEIGHT/ID: 75cm. Erect-branched shrub. Leaves hairy, linear and sword-shaped, up to 6cm long and 5cm wide.

FLOWERS: Globular and papery, up to 6cm across. Can be pale pink, pink or red. Flowers in autumn and winter.

HABITAT/RANGE: Common among native grasses and along roadsides in Northern Territory, Western Australia and Queensland.

Tall Sundew *Drosera auriculata*

HEIGHT/ID: 30cm. Insectivorous, mostly erect herb. Height variable. Leaves nearly circular and form a flat rosette. Long hairs on leaves have sticky droplets at tips to trap insects.

FLOWERS: White or pink, usually 1.5cm across. Sepals hairless. Flowers from winter to spring.

HABITAT/RANGE: Common in damp areas and moist sandy bushland in South Australia, Victoria, Tasmania, New South Wales and south-east Queensland.

Grampians Bauera *Bauera sessiliflora*

HEIGHT/ID: 2m. Tall and erect bushy shrub with hairy branches. Leaves divided into three oblong leaflets, up to 2.5cm.

FLOWERS: Magenta or pink with five small open petals and usually crowded into a small cluster. Stalkless with numerous black-tipped stamens. Flowers in spring.

HABITAT/RANGE: Sheltered sandy low areas or swamps. Endemic to the Grampians of Victoria.

Pink-bells *Tetratheca ciliata*

HEIGHT/ID: 90cm. A small and slender shrub with a number of hairy ridged branches. Leaves alternate and fringed with hairs.

FLOWERS: From lilac to pink or red, seldom white, and 2.5cm wide. Always has dark brown centre, either eight or ten stamens and four spreading petals. Flowers mainly in spring.

HABITAT/RANGE: Grows in most sandy soils, heathlands and forest regions of New South Wales, Queensland, South Australia and Tasmania.

Upside-down Plant *Leptosema chambersii*

HEIGHT/ID: 70cm. A small leafless shrub with a tangle of grey-green stems.

FLOWERS: The long red flowers have red stamens. They grow at the base of the plant, resting on the soil. Flowers in winter.

HABITAT/RANGE: Desert areas of Northern Territory, South Australia and Western Australia.

Green Birdflower *Crotalaria cunninghamii*

HEIGHT/ID: 2m. Erect shrub with high branches. Stems feel leathery. Leaves are egg-shaped, hairy, velvet to touch and grow up to 8cm long.

FLOWERS: Pea-shaped and usually green, sometimes yellow. They are streaked with thin black lines and grow to 4cm long. Racemes can be over 20cm long. Flowers from winter to spring.

HABITAT/RANGE: Grows in sandy inland habitats in South Australia, Western Australia, Northern Territory, Queensland and New South Wales.

Running Postman *Kennedia prostrata*

HEIGHT/ID: Prostrate. A creeping shrub that can cover up to 5m in area. Leaves formed of three leaflets, circular and partly egg-shaped, up to 3cm long.

FLOWERS: Bright red and pea-shaped with small yellow centre. Can grow individually or in pairs. Flowers from winter to spring.

HABITAT/RANGE: In a variety of soils and conditions, including open forests, heathlands and sandy-clay areas in Western Australia, South Australia, Victoria, Tasmania and New South Wales.

Cockies' Tongues *Templetonia retusa*

HEIGHT/ID: 1.5m. Mainly erect shrub, but can be prostrate, with very rigid branches. Grey-green leaves are often leathery, oblong and broaden towards tip.

FLOWERS: Mainly deep red, but can be white or pink-purple. Up to 4cm long, pea-shaped with a curled-back petal and a long and narrow keel arranged in a small auxiliary cluster. Flowers winter to spring.

HABITAT/RANGE: Sandy soils, open heathlands, forests and mallee country of South Australia and Western Australia.

Sturt's Desert Pea *Swainsona formosa*

HEIGHT/ID: Prostrate. Spreading annual or perennial plant with thick upright stems covered in fine hairs. Grey-green leaves up to 15cm long and divided into narrow 3cm-long oblong leaflets.

FLOWERS: Bright red pea-shaped flower up to 8cm long. Pointed with erect racemes and a large raised glossy black spot at the base. Flowers at almost any time after rain. Floral emblem of South Australia.

HABITAT/RANGE: Dry inland areas of all mainland states except Victoria.

Matted Bush-pea *Pultenaea pedunculata*

HEIGHT/ID: Prostrate form. Habitat varies greatly with this plant, often the prostrate stems will take root. Leaves are crowded; they are narrow and grow to 1cm long.

FLOWERS: Small yellow flowers on thread-like stems, can be up to 2cm long and are conspicuous in the bush. Flowers can be orange or yellow. Flowers in spring.

HABITAT/RANGE: Dry bushland areas of Victoria, South Australia, New South Wales and Tasmania.

Dwarf Wedge-pea *Gompholobium ecostatum*

HEIGHT/ID: 30cm. Erect or sometimes a spreading shrub. Leaves have three linear leaflets that grow to 1cm long.

FLOWERS: Pea-shaped, varying from deep apricot to red with a yellow centre. Flower can be solitary or in pairs. Flowers from spring to summer.

HABITAT/RANGE: Sandy soils and open forest areas of Victoria and South Australia.

Common Wedge-pea *Gompholobium huegelii*

HEIGHT/ID: 30cm. A herbaceous and scrambling plant. Leaves have three linear leaflets up to 10cm long and 1cm wide; these are on the stems of the plant.

FLOWERS: Yellow pea-shaped blooms very uniform in size and colour. Flowers in spring.

HABITAT/RANGE: Prefers the sandy and gravelly areas and open bushland regions of Tasmania. Victoria and New South Wales.

Narrow-leaf Bitter-pea *Daviesia leptophylla*

HEIGHT/ID: 2m. A broom-like shrub. Oval-shaped leaves up to 6cm long and bitter to taste.

FLOWERS: Golden-yellow, sometimes yellow and brown, pea flowers. Flowers occupy very dense racemes. Flowers late spring to summer.

HABITAT/RANGE: Open bushland and forest areas of Victoria, New South Wales and Tasmania.

Common Flat-pea *Platylobium obtusangulum*

HEIGHT/ID: 1m. Erect, spreading shrub with wiry branches. Leaves triangular and pointed, up to 3cm long.

FLOWERS: Pea-shaped flowers are orange-yellow with red-brown centres and overlapping bracts. Some are single, others in clumps of two or three. Flowers in spring.

HABITAT/RANGE: Common in heathland and open forest areas of South Australia, Victoria and Tasmania.

Showy Parrot-pea *Dillwynia sericea*

HEIGHT/ID: 1m. Tall erect shrub, stem usually covered with white silky hairs, more often when plant is young. Linear leaves grow to 2cm.

FLOWERS: Pea-shaped flowers about 1.5cm across and golden-yellow, or can be orange with some red markings. Flowers are often in pairs on the upper leaf axils. Flowers in winter and spring.

HABITAT/RANGE: Widespread in heathlands and open forest areas of southern South Australia, Victoria, Tasmania, New South Wales and south-east Queensland.

Swan River Pea *Brachysema celsianum*

HEIGHT/ID: 1.5m. A small spreading shrub which will climb if possible. Stems have silvery hairs. Leaves sword-like in appearance, dark green and smooth, can grow to 10cm.

FLOWERS: Pea-shaped and red, grow to about 2.5cm long and are usually solitary, sometimes in a cluster of two or three. Flowers from winter to spring.

HABITAT/RANGE: Areas of mallee scrubland in Western Australia.

Fire Bush *Senna pleurocarpa*

HEIGHT/ID: 1.5m. Very sprawling and hairless shrub. It will also sucker if conditions suit. Leaves are divided and up to 17cm long.

FLOWERS: Yellow flowers usually 1.6cm across; they are erect and have spike-like racemes. Flowers at any time of the year when conditions suit.

HABITAT/RANGE: In the sandy areas of all mainland Australia except Victoria.

Mudgee Wattle *Acacia spectabilis*

HEIGHT/ID: 2m. Erect shrub, stem often hangs in a drooping fashion and covered with thick hairs. Blue-green leaves are divided, oblong and pointed at tip.

FLOWERS: Golden-yellow, the globular heads are on long racemes which can measure 15cm. Flowers from winter to spring.

HABITAT/RANGE: In areas of forest and bushland of north-east New South Wales and south-east Queensland.

West Wyalong Wattle *Acacia cardiophylla*

HEIGHT/ID: 3m. A bushy shrub with finely divided, soft green fern-like foliage; each leaflet is about 2cm long. Has long arching branches that become covered with flowers.

FLOWERS: The branches are a mass of spiky yellow balls in spring. Flowers from winter to spring.

HABITAT/RANGE: A mallee country species of New South Wales.

Sydney Golden Wattle *Acacia longifolia*

HEIGHT/ID: 8m. Erect and spreading tree. Has flattened stalks that double as leaves (phyllodes); these can be up to 20cm long.

FLOWERS: Golden yellow in a spike up to 20cm long. Flowers from winter to spring.

HABITAT/RANGE: Coastal areas and mountain ranges of New South Wales, Victoria and south-east South Australia.

Witchetty Bush *Acacia kempeana*

HEIGHT/ID: 3m. Erect and a spreading shrub, the phyllodes are flattened and slightly curled, growing to 10cm long and 1.5cm wide; small veins run through and the tip is rounded.

FLOWERS: Golden-yellow flowers in spikes and about 3cm long. Flowers from winter to spring.

HABITAT/RANGE: Widespread in the dry areas of Queensland, South Australia, Western Australia and Northern Territory.

Queensland Silver Wattle *Acacia podalyriifolia*

HEIGHT/ID: 4 m. Erect shrub, stems often hairy. Phyllodes flat, almost egg-shaped and up to 3cm long and 2cm wide; usually silver-grey.

FLOWERS: Golden-yellow flowers in a globular head, set on slender stalk on stem. Flowers from winter to spring.

HABITAT/RANGE: Mainly coastal areas of New South Wales and Queensland; also locally in Victoria and Western Australia.

Flat Wattle *Acacia glaucoptera*

HEIGHT/ID: 1m. Well branched and rounded shrub. Unusual flat grey leaf-like stems overlap continuously in zigzagged pattern. New growth often red or bronze.

FLOWERS: Yellow balls emerge from central stem during spring.

HABITAT/RANGE: Well-drained areas of forest and bush in Western Australia and New South Wales.

Grey Mulga *Acacia brachybotrya*

HEIGHT/ID: 1m. A spreading shrub, the stem is covered with small hairs. Phyllodes green, egg-shaped and up to 4cm long with rounded tip.

FLOWERS: Bright yellow with globular heads. Can be in clusters or sometimes single-headed on the stem. Flowers from winter to spring.

HABITAT/RANGE: The dry inland regions of mainly the mallee areas of New South Wales, Victoria and South Australia.

Sword-leaf Wattle *Acacia gladiiformis*

HEIGHT/ID: 3m. Evergreen. Stem is shrub-like with angular branches. Phyllodes are leathery and curved, rigid and narrow.

FLOWERS: Flowers are golden balls which occur in loose sprays on the stems. Flowers in spring.

HABITAT/RANGE: Thrives in most soils in the New South Wales area.

Painted Featherflower *Verticordia picta*

HEIGHT/ID: 1m. Small shrub. Leaves long and narrow and usually grow to 1cm.

FLOWERS: Pink or purple, up to 1.2cm across with rounded petals and feather-like sepals. They are profuse and grow in loose clusters. Flowers in spring.

HABITAT/RANGE: Open bushland areas of southern and western Western Australia.

Yellow Featherflower *Verticordia chrysantha*

HEIGHT/ID: 80cm. Small erect shrub. Leaves linear, slender and pointed at tip.

FLOWERS: Yellow, up to 1.5cm across. Grow profusely in loose clusters. Feather-like petals heavily fringed. Flowers in spring.

HABITAT/RANGE: Heathlands and sand plains of Western Australia.

Woolly Featherflower *Verticordia monadelpha*

HEIGHT/ID: 1m. Thick and bushy shrub. Leaves up to 3cm long but not seen when bush in flower.

FLOWERS: Mass of feathery pink to lilac-purple flowers, up to 8cm across. Flowers mainly in spring.

HABITAT/RANGE: Clay and sandy soils in Geraldton area of Western Australia.

Roe's Featherflower *Verticordia roei*

HEIGHT/ID: 45cm. Small tightly cropped shrub, no leaves or limbs visible when in flower.

FLOWERS: Mainly tight clusters of white flowers, about 1cm across. All of the flowers open simultaneously. Flowers from early spring to early summer.

HABITAT/RANGE: Light sandy soils and gravelly areas of southern Western Australia.

Verticordia sp. *Verticordia etheliana*

HEIGHT/ID: 30cm. Small perennial herb. Leaves 2–3cm long, flat and smooth and almost round.

FLOWERS: Brilliant red flowers grow from stems, they have long tips to 4–5cm long and a feathery rosette of petals. Flowers in spring.

HABITAT/RANGE: Sandy areas and open heaths in Geraldton area of Western Australia.

Verticordia sp. *Verticordia oculata*

HEIGHT/ID: 70cm. Low-growing, sprawling shrub. Several stems emerge from the one main plant.

FLOWERS: Flowers and stem leaves all circular, with white margin attached directly to the stem; flowers up to 1cm long and have to 14 white lobes. Flowers grouped like a spreading arrangement near the upper area of the stem. Flowers in summer.

HABITAT/RANGE: Sandy heathlands in Geraldton area of Western Australia.

Swamp Paperbark *Melaleuca ericifolia*

HEIGHT/ID: 6m. Small tree or shrub with greyish trunk. Alternate leaves can be 1–2cm long – they are narrow, linear and often the tip is curved at the end.

FLOWERS: Usually white to off-white, rarely any other color. Flowers crowded in heads or sometimes in short spikes up to 2.5cm long; these grow into leafy shoots. Stamens creamy-white. Flowers from spring to summer.

HABITAT/RANGE: Heathlands and sandy areas in New South Wales, Victoria and Tasmania.

Bracelet Honey-myrtle *Melaleuca armillaris*

HEIGHT/ID: 5m. Shrub or small tree with firm bark and grey trunk. Leaves linear, up to 2.5cm long and 1cm wide, with pointed tips.

FLOWERS: Cylinder-shaped white flowers. Flowers from spring to summer.

HABITAT/RANGE: Widespread over heathlands and tablelands of New South Wales, Victoria, South Australia and areas of Tasmania and south-west Western Australia.

Melaleuca sp. *Melaleuca thymoides*

HEIGHT/ID: 2m. A small shrub with sword-like leaves which are 1–3cm long.

FLOWERS: Small yellow flower-heads, mainly at ends of stiff limbs. Flowers in spring and summer.

HABITAT/RANGE: Sandy areas and open heathlands of south-west Western Australia.

Chenille Honey-myrtle *Melaleuca huegelii*

HEIGHT/ID: 3m. Shrub with triangular leaves, which are small and crowded against the stems. Makes a good windbreak – can be cut to form windbreaks if needed.

FLOWERS: Flowers in spikes up to 10cm long. Red petals often hidden when flowering by pink or white stamen bundles. Flowers late spring to early summer.

HABITAT/RANGE: Coastal and limestone areas of Western Australia.

Corky Honey-myrtle *Melaleuca suberosa*

HEIGHT/ID: 70cm. Very unusual shrub with linear leaves up to 1cm long. Has thick corky bark on trunk.

FLOWERS: Flowers appear to emerge through the bark along the length of a stem and can be lilac, pink or red. Flowers spring to summer.

HABITAT/RANGE: Sandy heathlands in southern Western Australia.

Totem Poles *Melaleuca decussata*

HEIGHT/ID: 5m. Erect shrub. Pointed bluish-green leaves are opposite each other, sometimes crowded on stem.

FLOWERS: Usually pale lilac and has five lobes with numerous protruding stamens all arranged in cylindrical hairy spikes. Flowers from spring to summer.

HABITAT/RANGE: Rocky areas and sandy flats, often near water or swamps, in Victoria and South Australia.

Scarlet Honey-myrtle *Melaleuca fulgens*

HEIGHT/ID: 2m. Erect and sprawling shrub. Leaves sword-shaped, pointed at tip and up to 3cm long.

FLOWERS: Usually red, sometimes orange or pink. Spikes up to 5cm long and 4cm wide. Flowers from spring to summer.

HABITAT/RANGE: Usually associated with wheat-growing areas of Western Australia.

Wiry Honey-myrtle *Melaleuca filifolia*

HEIGHT/ID: 2m. Erect shrub. Thin slender leaves are up to 3cm long and 15cm wide, slightly curved and pointed. Formerly known as *M. nematophylla*.

FLOWERS: Purple-mauve with golden anthers. Rounded terminal flower-heads about 5cm in diameter. Spring flowering.

HABITAT/RANGE: Open sand plains of Western Australia.

Wilson's Honey-myrtle *Melaleuca wilsonii*

HEIGHT/ID: 1.2m. Dense shrub, can be prostrate at times. Narrow pointed leaves have a citrus scent when crushed.

FLOWERS: Usually pink-lilac, sometimes white. Flowers bloom along the branches in dense clusters. Flowers from spring to summer.

HABITAT/RANGE: Semi-arid areas of Victoria and South Australia.

Prickly Paperbark *Melaleuca styphelioides*

HEIGHT/ID: 20m. A small shrub with papery bark. Bright green leaves are about 2cm long, slightly twisted and egg-shaped with a sharp tip.

FLOWERS: Profuse white flowers in cylindrical clumps up to 3cm long. Flowers from spring to summer.

HABITAT/RANGE: Coastal areas and swampland mainly in New South Wales, also locally in Victoria and south-east Queensland.

Prickly-leaved Paperbark *Melaleuca nodosa*

HEIGHT/ID: 1.2m. Erect shrub with papery bark on trunk. Leaves slender, sharply pointed and rigid, up to 3cm long.

FLOWERS: Pale yellow with globular flower-heads up to 1.5cm across. Flowers from spring to summer.

HABITAT/RANGE: Widespread on coastal and sandy heathlands of Queensland and New South Wales.

Broombush *Melaleuca uncinata*

HEIGHT/ID: 2m. Erect and multi-stemmed shrub with papery bark on trunk. Slender leaves grow to 6cm long; tips pointed and slightly recurved.

FLOWERS: Flowers usually pale yellow or light cream and grow in globular heads which are about 1.5cm across and often terminal. Flowers from winter to spring.

HABITAT/RANGE: Dry inland regions of all mainland states. Often grows among the mallee eucalypt trees.

Melaleuca sp. *Melaleuca pentagona*

HEIGHT/ID: 3m. Erect shrub. Leaves are needle-like and pointed, up to 2cm long.

FLOWERS: Pink and in tight clusters on the stems, with pale golden tips on ends of flower-heads.

HABITAT/RANGE: Sandy heathlands and open forest areas in Western Australia.

Granite Honey-myrtle *Melaleuca elliptica*

HEIGHT/ID: 2.5m. Erect shrub. Grey bark is slippery and papery. Leaves 1.5cm long, flat with rounded tip.

FLOWERS: Red cylindrical spikes up to 8cm long and 5cm across on older stems. Flowers from spring to summer.

HABITAT/RANGE: Granite areas of southern Western Australia.

Rough Honey-myrtle *Melaleuca scabra*

HEIGHT/ID: 1–2m. Small spreading shrub. Leaves 1cm long and linear with very prominent point on tip.

FLOWERS: Deep pink to purple in terminal heads about 1cm across. Flowers from spring to summer.

HABITAT/RANGE: Widespread in heath and forest areas of Western Australia.

Graceful Honey-myrtle *Melaleuca radula*

HEIGHT/ID: 1.5m. Spreading shrub. Leaves long and narrow, up to 5cm long, pointed at tip and glandular.

FLOWERS: Pink or purple spikes up to 2.5cm long on short stem. Flowers from winter to spring.

HABITAT/RANGE: Coastal areas and open heathlands of Western Australia.

Showy Honey-myrtle *Melaleuca nesophila*

HEIGHT/ID: 2m. Bush-shaped shrub with papery bark on trunk. Leathery leaves 2cm long and oblong with rounded tip which may have a small point.

FLOWERS: Mauve to purple globular terminal head up to 3cm across. Flowers from winter to spring.

HABITAT/RANGE: Sandy coastal regions of Western Australia.

Robin Red-breast Bush *Melaleuca lateritia*

HEIGHT/ID: 1.5m. Multi-stemmed and open bush. Leaves thin, flat, up to 2cm long and pointed at tip.

FLOWERS: Orange to red 8cm-long spikes on short stems, usually on old wood. Flowers from spring to summer.

HABITAT/RANGE: Widespread in the mallee areas and heathland of Western Australia.

Green-flowered Paperbark *Melaleuca viridiflora*

HEIGHT/ID: 6m. Small tree with grey to cream trunks. Trunk very fibrous and bark in layers. Dull dark green leaves are broad, oval, flat, stiff, smooth and 15cm long.

FLOWERS: Usually pale greenish-yellow, can also be red. Dense cylindrical flower spikes, often in small groups. Flowers mainly in spring.

HABITAT/RANGE: Grows well in most soils, but prefers heavy clay, in Northern Territory, Queensland and north-east Western Australia.

Violet Kunzea *Kunzea parvifolia*

HEIGHT/ID: 2.5m. Tall and erect shrub, slender in appearance with wiry branches. Dull green leaves small and stalkless, oblong, spear-like and curled with black tips; can be 4mm long and 1mm wide. Small glands on each leaf.

FLOWERS: Pinkish flowers 4–5mm wide with five small lobes and numerous long stamens. Small terminal heads are about 10cm wide.

HABITAT/RANGE: Elevated areas of New South Wales, Queensland and Victoria.

Baxter's Kunzea *Kunzea baxteri*

HEIGHT/ID: 1.5m. Spreading shrub with many stems. Leaves linear and oblong, up to 1.5cm long and often edged with tiny white hairs.

FLOWERS: Usually deep red. Dense cylindrical spikes about 2.5cm long are prominent. Stamens can be 10cm long and tipped with white or cream. Spring flowering.

HABITAT/RANGE: Granite country and coastal areas of southern Western Australia.

Tick Bush *Kunzea ambigua*

HEIGHT/ID: To 3m. Spreading shrub. Dark green leaves are narrow, pointed at tip and up to 1cm long.

FLOWERS: About 1.5cm wide and nearly always white. Stamens white and longer than petals. Flowers in spring.

HABITAT/RANGE: Coastal areas and heathlands of Tasmania, Victoria and New South Wales.

Pink Bottlebrush *Beaufortia schaueri*

HEIGHT/ID: 1m. Small-branched shrub. Leaves narrow, linear, pointed at tip, up to 3cm long and crowded.

FLOWERS: Can be lilac or pink. Flower-heads rounded and about 2cm across. Flowers at ends of short lateral branches. Flowers from winter to spring.

HABITAT/RANGE: Sandy heathlands and gravelly areas of southern Western Australia.

Stirling Range Bottlebrush *Beaufortia heterophylla*

HEIGHT/ID: 1m. Small-leaved and twiggy shrub. Leaves very hair-like in appearance; can grow to 10cm long.

FLOWERS: Flowers bright scarlet or purplish-red. Flower spikes clustered along branches. Prominent stamens up to 2.5cm long. Flowers winter to spring.

HABITAT/RANGE: Gravelly soil, open woodlands and heath country of north-east Western Australia.

Ravensthorpe Bottlebrush *Beaufortia orbifolia*

HEIGHT/ID: 3m. Small shrub. Leaves up to 2cm long. Small woody fruits crowded in spikes along stems.

FLOWERS: Flower spikes up to 4cm in diameter; they are bicoloured at first, then turn deep red. Flowers from winter to early summer.

HABITAT/RANGE: Open forest areas and roadsides of southern Western Australia.

Sand Bottlebrush *Beaufortia squarrosa*

HEIGHT/ID: 2m. Erect and spreading shrub. Leaves usually in pairs and can be 5cm long.

FLOWERS: Usually bright red, sometimes orange-yellow, in tufted spikes up to 3cm long. Flowers from spring to autumn.

HABITAT/RANGE: Sandy plains and heathlands of Western Australia.

Swamp Bottlebrush *Beaufortia sparsa*

HEIGHT/ID: 1.2m. Erect, open, spreading shrub. Leaves crowded and scattered along branch; they are egg-shaped with a pointed tip and some have curved-back margins.

FLOWERS: Red to orange cylindrical spikes up to 7cm long. Stamens wide and drooping. Flowers in summer.

HABITAT/RANGE: Swampy areas of sand plains and heathlands of south-west Western Australia.

Lemon Bottlebrush *Callistemon pallidus*

HEIGHT/ID: 3m. Stiff and erect shrub. Young growth usually has silky hairs on branches. Leaves stiff, leathery, narrow, pointed and up to 7cm long and 2cm wide.

FLOWERS: Cream to greenish-yellow spikes up to 7cm long and 3.5cm wide. Numerous long protruding stamens arranged in cylindrical spikes up to 9cm long. Flowers from spring to summer.

HABITAT/RANGE: Damp water courses and sandy heathlands of Tasmania, Victoria, New South Wales and south-east Queensland.

Scarlet Bottlebrush *Callistemon rugulosus*

HEIGHT/ID: 4m. Spreading and very branching shrub with some prickles on trunk. Leaves alternate and are narrow, sharply pointed and up to 8cm long. Oil glands in leaves are prominent.

FLOWERS: Bright red with numerous yellow-tipped stamens arranged through the cylindrical flower spike. Flowers in spring.

HABITAT/RANGE: Sandy to swampy soils in mallee and open forest land of Victoria and South Australia.

Wallum Bottlebrush *Callistemon pachyphyllus*

HEIGHT/ID: 1.5m. Spreading and open shrub. Thick, dull green leaves are narrow with pointed tip; up to 9cm long and 1cm wide.

FLOWERS: Bright red or green flower spikes 10cm long and 6cm wide. Flowers from spring to summer.

HABITAT/RANGE: Damp sandy areas of New South Wales and Queensland.

Stiff Bottlebrush *Callistemon rigidus*

HEIGHT/ID: 2.5m. Erect and a vigorous shrub. Young growth has silky hairs on stems. Leaves are linear with pointed tips; up to 7cm long.

FLOWERS: Red spiky flowers up to 10cm long and 6cm wide. Flowers from spring to summer.

HABITAT/RANGE: Coastal regions of New South Wales.

Dwarf Bottlebrush *Callistemon subulatus*

HEIGHT/ID: 1.8m. Small spreading shrub with arching branches. Leaves linear with very pointed tips, partly cylindrical and up to 5cm long.

FLOWERS: Red spikes up to 8cm long and 5cm wide, often in clusters at ends of branches. Flowers from spring to summer.

HABITAT/RANGE: Coastal and some tableland areas of New South Wales and Victoria.

Prickly Bottlebrush *Callistemon brachyandrus*

HEIGHT/ID: 5m. Tall and erect spreading shrub. Leaves stiff, needle-sharp, pointed and grooved.

FLOWERS: Orange to red with five small lobes and numerous 1cm-long yellow-tipped stamens. Cylindrical spikes 3–5cm long. Flowers from spring.

HABITAT/RANGE: Creek beds and open forest areas of New South Wales, Victoria and South Australia.

Oldfield's Darwinia *Darwinia oldfieldii*

HEIGHT/ID: 1m. Small shrub with numerous short stems. Leaves mainly oblong; margins fringed and usually recurved.

FLOWERS: Deep red, often 10 or more flower-heads with long styles and very short bracts. Flowers from winter to spring.

HABITAT/RANGE: Mainly in Murchison River district of Western Australia.

Geraldton Wax *Chamelaucium uncinatum*

HEIGHT/ID: 1m. Very erect shrub with many long, slender branches. Leaves scented and linear with hairless tip and hooked point.

FLOWERS: Small terminal clusters. Open-petalled, 2.5cm across with wax-like appearance. Can be white, mauve or pink. Flowers from winter to spring.

HABITAT/RANGE: Sandplains and open areas, usually north of Perth in Kalbarri district.

Turkey Bush *Calytrix exstipulata*

HEIGHT/ID: 3m. Erect and bushy. Stems short and numerous. Three-sided leaves are long and crowded on stem.

FLOWERS: Deep pink and star-like. Can be white or pale pink to purple. Flowers profusely in clusters from autumn to winter.

HABITAT/RANGE: Woodland and open forest country in tropical regions of Queensland, Northern Territory and Western Australia.

Shiny Tea-tree *Leptospermum nitidum*

HEIGHT/ID: 3m. Erect and spreading shrub. Shiny green leaves are 7cm long, knife-shaped and pointed at tip.

FLOWERS: 3cm across with five separate white lobes around a green central disc and surrounded by many stamens. Flowers from spring to summer.

HABITAT/RANGE: Coastal areas and heathlands of Victoria and Tasmania.

Lilac Hibiscus *Alyogyne huegelii*

HEIGHT/ID: 2m. Erect shrub with rigid hairy branches. Leaves up to 7cm long and divided; lobes irregularly shaped and hairy on both sides.

FLOWERS: Lilac to pink, rarely white. Up to 12cm wide with five overlapping petals. Centre has yellow, star-like protruding style. Flowers spring to summer.

HABITAT/RANGE: Variety of habitats in South Australia and Western Australia.

Yellow Hibiscus *Hibiscus panduriformis*

HEIGHT/ID: 1.2m. Erect and open shrub; stems very hairy. Leaves egg-shaped with slight toothing and up to 9cm long and 8cm wide. Grey-green on top, much paler underneath.

FLOWERS: Solitary yellow flower with maroon centre, up to 12cm across. Flowers at any time of year when conditions suit.

HABITAT/RANGE: Clay-pan areas and savanna woodlands in Queensland, Northern Territory and Western Australia.

Sturt's Desert Rose *Gossypium sturtianum*

HEIGHT/ID: 2m. Dense shrub. Stem often has black spots. Leaves alternate and egg-shaped; can be 6cm long and 2cm wide.

FLOWERS: Flowers pink or lilac with dark red centre, 5–10cm across with five overlapping rounded lobes. Flowers after good rains at any time of year. Floral emblem of the Northern Territory.

HABITAT/RANGE: Arid dry areas, mainly in central Australia. Found in all mainland states.

Round-leaf Rice-flower *Pimelea nivea*

HEIGHT/ID: 2m. Erect and spreading shrub, branches usually covered with dense white hairs. Leaves flat and oval, partly rounded and grow to 1.5cm; they are dark green and glossy above, nearly white underneath.

FLOWERS: Either white or pale pink, usually in dense terminal heads, 3cm long. Often has slight perfume. Flowers from spring to summer.

HABITAT/RANGE: Widespread in open forest areas of Tasmania.

Qualup Bell *Pimelea physodes*

HEIGHT/ID: 1m. Slender shrub, very erect. Blue-green leaves narrow, oval, flat and 1–3cm long with prominent tip.

FLOWERS: Greenish-yellow and fully enclosed in bracts that form a bell-like pendent. Flower-head up to 6cm long. Flowers from winter to spring.

HABITAT/RANGE: Sandy heathland and forests of Western Australia.

Rose Banjine *Pimelea rosea*

HEIGHT/ID: 1m. Erect, slender shrub. Leaves broad and pointed, 1–2cm long and 6mm across.

FLOWERS: White to rose pink. Terminal heads up to 4cm across. Flowers from winter to summer.

HABITAT/RANGE: Coastal plains of southern Western Australia.

Common Correa *Correa reflexa*

HEIGHT/ID: Up to 2m, but usually 1m. Can be erect shrub or spreading plant. Leaves opposite and pear-shaped.

FLOWERS: Red or cream bell-shaped flowers up to 4cm long with pale (greenish, yellowish or whitish) tips. Up to eight protruding stamens hang from inside flower. Flowers from winter to spring.

HABITAT/RANGE: Found in all states except Western Australia, in a wide variety of habitats.

Forest Boronia *Boronia muelleri*

HEIGHT/ID: 3m. Branches often glandular. Leaves divided and up to 5cm long. Can have many oval, flat leaves which are finely toothed with pointed tips.

FLOWERS: Pale pink flowers with four spreading petals, 2cm across and in clusters of to seven in the axils. Flowers profusely at times. Winter flowering.

HABITAT/RANGE: Mainly coastal areas of Victoria and New South Wales.

Pink Swamp-heath *Sprengelia incarnata*

HEIGHT/ID: 1m. Upright shrub. Leaves up to 2cm long and wrap around the stem.

FLOWERS: Clusters of pink or off-white flowers grow profusely from stem. Flowers from winter to spring.

HABITAT/RANGE: In a variety of soils in New South Wales, Victoria and Tasmania.

Curry Flower *Lysinema ciliatum*

HEIGHT/ID: 70cm. Small slender shrub with egg-shaped leaves up to 6cm long. Leaves can be curry scented.

FLOWERS: White star-shaped flowers up to 2cm long, with brown sepals and dense bracts. Flowers from winter to spring.

HABITAT/RANGE: Sandy soils and gravelly areas of southern Western Australia.

Common Heath *Epacris impressa*

HEIGHT/ID: Up to 2m, usually 1m. Usually tall and erect. Leaves attached to plant stem, often crowded on stem, and are sharply pointed; they can be 15mm long and 6mm wide.

FLOWERS: Stem often crowded with pink or red (sometimes white) bell-shaped flowers on short stalks and arranged in small clusters. Flowers from autumn to spring. The floral emblem of Victoria.

HABITAT/RANGE: Wet or damp areas in heathland or bush in Tasmania, Victoria, eastern New South Wales and south-east South Australia.

Fuchsia Heath *Epacris longiflora*

HEIGHT/ID: 2.2m. Straggling shrub with wiry stalk and hairy branches. The few leaves are bare and almost heart-shaped with rigid spear-like points.

FLOWERS: Red flowers are tubular and up to 3cm long with either brown or white tips. Each petal is singular on stem. Flowers autumn to spring.

HABITAT/RANGE: Flowers almost year-round in coastal areas and tablelands of Victoria, New South Wales and south-east Queensland.

Candle Heath *Richea continentis*

HEIGHT/ID: 1m. Small branched shrub. Stems spread and often take root. Leaves pointed and 2–4cm long with crowded sheath at the base of plant.

FLOWERS: Creamy-white, egg-shaped and nearly 2cm long. Flowers from summer.

HABITAT/RANGE: Alpine and sub-alpine regions of New South Wales and Victoria.

Golden Heath *Styphelia adscendens*

HEIGHT/ID: 40cm. Dense-growing bush with greyish spine-tipped leaves up to 3cm long.

FLOWERS: Yellow to cream tubular flowers at ends of branches; 2–3cm long. The five loose hairy petals appear to roll backwards. Flowers from late winter to spring.

HABITAT/RANGE: Open heathland and bush areas of Victoria, Tasmania and New South Wales.

Flame Heath *Styphelia behrii*

HEIGHT/ID: 40cm. Often in small groups. Leaves flat and pointed.

FLOWERS: Tubular flowers usually red, but can be pink, yellow, cream or green. Flowers from late winter to summer.

HABITAT/RANGE: Heathland and open forest areas of New South Wales, Victoria and South Australia.

Snake-bush *Hemiandra pungens*

HEIGHT/ID: 1m. Usually a spreading plant, but also prostrate in some areas. Leaves fleshy and stiff, usually pointed, mostly flat or concave, up to 12cm long.

FLOWERS: White to mauve-pink, usually with red spots inside. Up to 2cm across with three lobes; upper and lower lips arranged in small auxiliary racemes. Flowers from spring to summer.

HABITAT/RANGE: Sandy heath areas of south-west Western Australia.

Rough Mint-bush *Prostanthera denticulata*

HEIGHT/ID: 1m. Very upright shrub. Leaves opposite, broad, slightly curled and up to 12mm long.

FLOWERS: Usually purple, tubular and up to 12mm long; arranged in pairs on slender leafy stem. Lower lip can be triple-lobed, while upper lip has two lobes. Flowers spring to summer.

HABITAT/RANGE: Gravelly or sandy areas of Victoria and New South Wales.

Fairy Aprons *Utricularia dichotoma*

HEIGHT/ID: 30cm. Erect shrub. An insectivorous herb. Leaves mainly submerged in water, finely divided and modified to trap small insects.

FLOWERS: Usually purple to lilac, sometimes white or yellow. Flowers are terminal, sometimes in small clusters. Flowers from spring to summer.

HABITAT/RANGE: Swamp areas, heathlands and other places with standing water. Found in all states except Northern Territory.

Crimson Turkey Bush *Eremophila latrobei*

HEIGHT/ID: 2m. Erect shrub. Stems warty and covered in fine hairs. Leaves narrow, up to 9cm long and 5cm wide.

FLOWERS: Tubular flowers up to 3cm long, mainly red, covered with fine hairs and with pointed lobes. Stamens extend a few cm beyond end of flower. Flowers from autumn to spring.

HABITAT/RANGE: Widespread in arid areas of all mainland states.

Wild Tomato *Solanum quadriloculatum*

HEIGHT/ID: 50cm. Sprawling shrub. Stems covered in dense hairs and prickles. Leaves egg-shaped and pointed at tip.

FLOWERS: Mainly purple with a yellow centre; 2.5cm across with pointed lobes. Flowers winter to spring.

HABITAT/RANGE: Widespread over much of Australia in a variety of soils. Occurs in all states except Victoria and Tasmania.

Poached Egg Daisy *Polycalymma stuartii*

HEIGHT/ID: 60cm. Erect woolly annual. Pointed grey-green leaves are 2.6cm long and 1.5mm wide, with veins running full length of leaf.

FLOWERS: Heads white with bright yellow centres about 2.5cm across. Flower-head feels papery. One flower per stem. Flowers from spring to summer or when rain falls.

HABITAT/RANGE: Sandy areas in dry, arid regions of Outback Australia.

Snow Daisy *Celmisia longifolia*

HEIGHT/ID: 30cm. Erect perennial. Very hairy silver leaves are linear or pear-shaped; they grow from base of plant, have curled-under margins and can be 25cm long.

FLOWERS: White with yellow centre, up to 2.5cm across. One flower per stem. Flowers from summer to autumn.

HABITAT/RANGE: Widespread in snow and high country of Tasmania, Victoria and New South Wales.

Fleshy Groundsel *Senecio gregorii*

HEIGHT/ID: 40cm. Very erect herb. Bluish-green leaves are thick, fleshy and pointed, growing to 2.9cm long.

FLOWERS: Brilliant bright yellow daisy-like flower. Solitary flower-head per stem. Flower-head about 5cm across with 8–12 florets. Flowers at any time, depending on rainfall.

HABITAT/RANGE: Widespread in arid mallee country of mainland Australia.

Minnie Daisy *Minuria leptophylla*

HEIGHT/ID: 50cm. Multi-branched. Narrow leaves up to 4cm long and 1cm wide; becoming smaller towards top.

FLOWERS: Petals vary from lilac to pink-purple, usually with a yellow centre. Can sometimes have up to 30 florets or petals.

HABITAT/RANGE: Widely distributed over much of Australia. In all states except Tasmania.

Pink Everlasting *Schoenia cassiniana*

HEIGHT/ID: 50cm. Small herb. Leaves sword-shaped, up to 7cm long and very densely covered with fine hairs. Some short leaves may occur on stem.

FLOWERS: Pink papery bract flowers with yellow centres in a terminal cluster. Each flower has about 10 tubular petals. Flowers in spring.

HABITAT/RANGE: Arid and semi-arid regions of South Australia, Western Australia and Northern Territory.

Spiked Dampiera *Dampiera spicigera*

HEIGHT/ID: 30cm. Erect perennial herb with many branches, usually grey or yellow and covered with hairs. Leaves oblong, toothed and up to 4cm long.

FLOWERS: Masses of blue flowers on leafless stems cover the entire plant. Flowers in spring.

HABITAT/RANGE: Heavy soils in south-west Western Australia.

Blue Leschenaultia *Lechenaultia biloba*

HEIGHT/ID: 80cm. Low and straggling shrub. Leaves needle-like and crowded, up to 1.5cm long; they are soft and feel partly fleshy.

FLOWERS: Delicate tubular flowers in various shades of blue. Up to 2cm long with five wedge-shaped lobes and hairy insides. Flowers from late winter to spring.

HABITAT/RANGE: Gravel areas of south-west Western Australia.

Red Leschenaultia *Lechenaultia formosa*

HEIGHT/ID: 50cm. Mainly prostrate shrub, stems may be spreading or partly erect. Fleshy leaves are linear, pointed, usually crowded and up to 1cm long.

FLOWERS: Colour variable but mainly in red. Flower 2–4mm across. Flowers from winter to spring.

HABITAT/RANGE: Southern coasts and hinterlands in Western Australia.

Fairy Fan-flower *Scaevola aemula*

HEIGHT/ID: 50cm. Sprawling perennial herb with ascending stems covered in yellow hairs. Leaves egg-shaped and slightly toothed, 2cm long and 4mm wide.

FLOWERS: From lilac to pink and spreading to one side like a fan, the terminal spikes are 24cm long. Flowers from spring to autumn.

HABITAT/RANGE: Coastal areas of New South Wales, Victoria, Queensland and South Australia.

Crab Claws *Stylidium macranthum*

HEIGHT/ID: 30cm. Erect shrub. Leaves are smooth and pointed, up to 30cm long.

FLOWERS: Flowers usually pink and resemble a crab's claw. Up to 2.5cm long.

HABITAT/RANGE: Sandy heaths and swamp areas in the Esperance area of Western Australia.

Grass Trigger-plant *Stylidium graminifolium*

HEIGHT/ID: 70cm. Upright perennial with long flowering stems. Leaves linear with curved margins and pointed tips; sometimes they are finely toothed, as well tufted at the base of the plant.

FLOWERS: Four spreading petals can be pink or magenta with a white centre. Unusual because has two stamens united in a long bent column, and when touched they spring closed. Spring and summer flowering.

HABITAT/RANGE: Dry forest areas, coastal regions and inland slopes in New South Wales, Queensland and Victoria.

GLOSSARY

Acute: having a sharp point.

Alternate: leaves on a stem, arranged at different levels, or not opposite each other.

Anther: pollen-bearing part of a stamen.

Axis: main part of a stem of a plant.

Bract: modified leaf structure that lacks a blade.

Calli: glands on labella of orchid which do not secrete.

Erect: plants that grow upright.

Floret: a small flower.

Foliage: the leaves of a plant.

Glabrous: smooth and without hairs.

Glandular: bearing glands or glandular hairs.

Habitat: the area or environment where plant grows.

Herbaceous: perennial plant that dies down after each flowering period.

Herb: plant used for medicine, food or scent.

Labellum: front petal of orchid.

Lanceolate: shaped like a lance and tapering at both ends.

Linear: long and narrow with both sides parallel.

Lobe: rounded part of leaf or petal.

Nectar: sweet fluid secreted from plant.

Oblong: leaf which is broader than it is long, with both ends rounded.

Obovate: egg-shaped with the broadest area in or above the middle.

Pendulous: hanging downwards.

Perennial: a plant that lives for more than two seasons.

Perfume: sweet scent, or a fragrant substance which emits an agreeable scent.

Petiole: the stalk of a leaf.

Phyllode: flat leaf or stalk.

Pinnate: leaves divided and arranged on each side of stalk, usually opposite each other.

Prostrate: plants that grow flat by creeping along the ground.

Pubescent: plants that are covered with short, soft or downy hairs

Pungent: leaves or plants that have a strong smell.

Recurved: leaves that curl downwards or backwards.

Raceme: unbranched cluster of flowers along a stem.

Rosette: leaves radiating in a circle from a central point.

Sac: a shallow pouch or cavity.

Sepal: leaf-like segment of the calyx.

Serrated: with sharp forward points.

Shoot: new growth from plant.

Spreading: plants that extend foliage.

Stamen: the male pollen-bearing organ of a flowering plant.

Style: long structure connecting stigma to ovary.

Succulent: with soft juicy flesh.

Sucker: new shoots appearing from main plant.

Terminal: situated at the end or top.

Terrestrial: growing in the ground.

Tuber: most orchids have a tuber or thickened roots.

Undulate: giving the appearance of waves.

Vein: structural tissues of a leaf, used to move water and minerals.

Viscous: sticky area of plant.

Winged: parts of the plant that are arranged on an axis.

INDEX

INDEX

OTHER TITLES IN THE SERIES

Reed Concise Guide: Animals of Australia (ISBN 978 1 92151 754 9)
Reed Concise Guide: Birds of Australia (ISBN 978 1 92151 753 2)